Animal Attacks

BEAR ATTACK

by Lisa Owings

BELLWETHER MEDIA · MINNEAPOLIS, MN

Are you ready to take it to the extreme? Torque books thrust you into the action-packed world of sports, vehicles, mystery, and adventure. These books may include dirt, smoke, fire, and dangerous stunts. WARNING: read at your own risk.

Library of Congress Cataloging-in-Publication Data

Owings, Lisa.
Bear attack / by Lisa Owings.
p. cm. -- (Torque: animal attacks)
Includes bibliographical references and index.
Summary: "Engaging images illustrate true bear attack stories and accompany survival tips. The combination of high-interest subject matter and light text is intended for students in grades 3 through 7" --Provided by publisher.
ISBN 978-1-60014-786-9 (hardcover : alk. paper)
ISBN 978-1-60014-843-9 (paperback : alk. paper)

1. Bear attacks--Juvenile literature. 2. Bears--Behavior--Juvenile literature. I. Title.
QL737.C27O968 2013
599.78--dc23

2012011220

This edition first published in 2013 by Bellwether Media, Inc.

Printed in the United States of America, North Mankato, MN.

TABLE OF CONTENTS

Brutal Bears

Coming face-to-face with a bear is a hiker's worst nightmare. Grizzlies and polar bears are the most feared. These giant **predators** are incredibly dangerous. Their jaws could crush a bowling ball. Their teeth and claws are made for shredding flesh. They will hunt you down if you try to run. And they will catch you.

Murderous Mamas

The deadliest bears are mother bears. They will attack anything they think might hurt their cubs.

True Survival Test

Seven teens hiked deep into the Alaskan wilderness. Mountain peaks rose above them as night approached. This was the last leg of a month-long survival course. The first in the group rounded a curve. Suddenly his scream pierced the air. "Bear! Bear!" The others turned and ran. But they could not outrun the angry grizzly **charging** after them.

Fast and Furious

Never run from a grizzly. These huge bears can reach speeds of up to 40 miles (64 kilometers) per hour.

The grizzly was on top of Josh Berg in seconds. The teen heard his skull crack. He went limp.

The bear kept moving. Sam Gottsegen glanced over his shoulder. The **snarling** grizzly was almost on him. It knocked him to the ground. He felt it tear open his chest. Its jaws locked on his head.

"I remember the jaws on my head and just thinking, *I'm going to die.*"

—Sam Gottsegen

"I heard noises around me and thought, *If this bear comes back, I won't make it.*"

—Sam Gottsegen

Victor Martin was the third **victim**. He was running when sharp teeth sank into his leg. He kicked the grizzly hard in the face. The bear finally ran off.

Others in the group bandaged the wounds and **signaled** for help. They feared their friends would die or the bear would return. Help arrived several hours later. The teens all lived to tell their stories.

Sam Gottsegen

The Longest Night

The teens waited more than five hours before a rescue helicopter came. Josh and Sam were too injured to be moved. They held on until a medical team came four hours later.

Polar Bear on the Prowl

It was early morning on the **Arctic** island of Spitsbergen. Eleven campers and their two leaders were asleep in their tents. A **trip wire** surrounded the camp. But no alarm sounded when a hungry polar bear entered. Sixteen-year-old Patrick Flinders woke up to a scratching sound. Then the bear ripped through his tent.

Hungry for Humans

Polar bears sometimes hunt people for food. This polar bear was thin and likely starving.

The polar bear brutally attacked another boy in Patrick's tent. Mike Reid and the other leader heard screaming and rushed to help. Mike aimed a gun at the bear, but the gun failed. The bear **mauled** both leaders. Then it turned its snapping jaws on Patrick. One bite crushed the bones in his arm. The next crunched into his skull.

"I wanted to hide but there was nowhere to go. I looked up and saw its huge mouth snapping. All around its nose was blood."

—Patrick Flinders

Patrick fought for his life. He punched the bear in the face. Suddenly the beast left the tent. It tackled another boy who had tried to run. A wounded Mike reloaded his gun and shot it. The bear was down at last. Those who survived were lucky. Their scars are permanent reminders of that day.

Patrick Flinders

A Bite to Remember

The injured campers were flown to a hospital after the attack. Doctors had to remove some of the polar bear's teeth from Patrick's cracked skull.

Prevent a Bear Attack

Being prepared in bear country can help prevent an attack. Always travel in groups. Make noise when hiking, especially if you cannot see far ahead. This warns bears to stay away and reduces your chance of surprising them. Keep food in sealed containers. The smell can attract bears. Carry **bear spray** with you at all times.

bear spray

The Usual Suspects
World's Most Dangerous Bears

Type	Range	Size
Polar bears	Arctic	900 to 1,600 pounds (410 to 725 kilograms)
Grizzly bears	North America	800 to 1,000 pounds (360 to 450 kilograms)
Brown bears (other than grizzlies)	Europe, Asia, and North America	300 to 800 pounds (135 to 360 kilograms)
Black bears	North America	200 to 600 pounds (90 to 270 kilograms)
Sloth bears	Asia	150 to 300 pounds (70 to 135 kilograms)

Be Bear Aware

Keep an eye out for bear tracks and scratches on trees. Signs of digging can also mean a bear is nearby.

Survive a Bear Attack

Most bears will steer clear of people. However, a startled bear, mother bear, or hungry bear may charge. If this happens, stand your ground. Running away invites the bear to chase after you.

You can try to scare a bear off by yelling or using bear spray. If it attacks, play dead until the bear loses interest. Hit the bear in the nose if it will not leave you alone. You have to be brave to survive a bear attack!

How to Use Bear Spray

- Wait until the bear is within about 30 feet (9 meters).
- Spray a cloud of mist toward the bear's face. Continue spraying until the bear stops or turns back.
- Back away. Keep the bear in sight as long as possible.

How to Play Dead

- Lie on your stomach or curl into a ball to protect your organs.
- Use your hands to cover your neck and head.
- Make sure the bear is long gone before you go for help.

Glossary

Arctic—the area around the North Pole

bear spray—a spray made from hot peppers; bear spray is used to stop bears from attacking.

charging—rushing forward to attack; bears often charge without attacking to scare off a threat.

mauled—attacked and injured with deep wounds

predators—animals that hunt other animals for food

signaled—used a sign or device to send a message or warning

snarling—growling with exposed teeth

trip wire—an alarm system used to alert campers when a dangerous animal comes near; trip wires are often hooked to devices that scare off animals with lights and noise.

victim—a person or animal that is hurt, killed, or made to suffer

To Learn More

AT THE LIBRARY

Hirschi, Ron. *Our Three Bears*. Honesdale, Pa.: Boyds Mills Press, 2008.

Owings, Lisa. *The Grizzly Bear*. Minneapolis, Minn.: Bellwether Media, 2012.

Rosing, Norbert, and Elizabeth Carney. *Face to Face with Polar Bears*. Washington, D.C.: National Geographic, 2007.

ON THE WEB

Learning more about bears is as easy as 1, 2, 3.

1. Go to www.factsurfer.com.
2. Enter "bears" into the search box.
3. Click the "Surf" button and you will see a list of related Web sites.

With factsurfer.com, finding more information is just a click away.

Index